Excel 2003

CW00400477

New CLAIT

Unit 4
Spreadsheets

Using
Microsoft® Excel 2003

Release NC024v1

Note: *Microsoft is a registered trademark and Windows is a trademark of the Microsoft Corporation.*

Published by:
  CiA Training Ltd
  Business & Innovation Centre
  Sunderland Enterprise Park
  Sunderland SR5 2TH
  United Kingdom
  Tel: +44 (0)191 549 5002
  Fax: +44 (0)191 549 9005
  info@ciatraining.co.uk
  www.ciatraining.co.uk

  ISBN 1 86005 212 6

© CiA Training Ltd 2004

New CLAIT   Excel 2003

CIA Training's guides for **New CLAIT** contain a collection of structured exercises to provide support for each unit in the new qualification. The exercises build into a complete open learning package covering the entire syllabus, to teach how to use a particular software application. They are designed to take the user through the features to enhance, fulfil and instil confidence in the product. The accompanying data disk enables the user to practise new techniques without the need for data entry.

This guide was created using version *2003* of *Excel* running under *Windows XP*. Some instructions may differ for users working with earlier versions of *Windows*. Where this is the case, instructions are added as notes. It is assumed that the computer is already switched on and that a printer and mouse are attached.

UNIT 4: SPREADSHEETS - The guide supporting this unit contains exercises covering the following topics:

- Spreadsheet Principles
- Formatting

- Screen and Worksheet
- Editing

- Menus
- Formulas

- Moving Around
- Copying

- Creating a Spreadsheet
- Cell Referencing

- Saving and Opening
- Printing

Visit www.ciasupport.co.uk for hints, tips and supplementary information on published CiA products.

This guide is suitable for:

- Any individual wishing to sit the OCR examination for this unit. The user works through the guide from start to finish.

- Tutor led groups as reinforcement material. It can be used as and when necessary.

Aim

To provide the knowledge and techniques necessary for the attainment of a certificate in this unit.

Objectives

After completing the guide the user will be able to:

- create spreadsheets

- format spreadsheets

- maintain spreadsheets

- print spreadsheets, formulas.

Introduction

This guide assumes that the program has been fully and correctly installed on your computer. However, in *Excel 2003,* some features are not initially installed and a prompt to insert the *Office 2003* CD may appear when these features are accessed.

Accompanying worksheets for the exercises are contained on disk. This avoids undue typing and speeds the learning process.

Important Notes For All Users

The disk accompanying this guide contains files. As the original data disk is to be reused, keep the master safe and always use a copy. Copy the master disk to a designated folder so that all newly created files can be saved to the same location. The data created during this guide will not fit on to a floppy disk.

Occasionally, long toolbars may be used and some of the buttons may be hidden. If this is the case, click on the chevrons at the right of the toolbar to reveal any hidden buttons.

When using menus, double click on the menu title to display the full range of commands.

Notation Used Throughout This Guide

- All key presses are included within < > e.g. <Enter> means press the **Enter** key. <Ctrl ↑> means hold down the Ctrl key and press the up arrow key. <End>↑ means press the End key and then press the up arrow key.

- Menu commands are written, e.g. **File | Open**.

- The guide is split into individual exercises. Each exercise consists of a written explanation of the feature, followed by a stepped exercise. Read the *Guidelines* and then follow the *Actions*, with reference to the Guidelines if necessary.

Recommendations

- It is suggested that users add their name, the date and exercise number after completing each exercise that requires a printed copy.

- Read the whole of each exercise before starting to work through it. This ensures understanding of the topic and prevents unnecessary mistakes.

Excel 2003   New CLAIT

Section 1

Fundamentals

By the end of this Section you should be able to:

Understand Spreadsheet Principles

Start Microsoft *Excel*

Understand the Screen Layout

Understand the Menus and Toolbars

Understand the Worksheet Window

Exit *Excel*

Exercise 1 - Spreadsheet Principles

Guidelines:

A spreadsheet package is a computer program created specifically to help in the processing of tabular information, usually numbers. The spreadsheet stores information in **rows** (across the screen) and **columns** (down the screen), forming a **Worksheet** (the *Excel* term for a spreadsheet). Several worksheets are bound together (three initially) to form a **Workbook**, the name *Excel* gives to a saved file.

Spreadsheets are most commonly used to manipulate figures. They can be used in:

Accounting

Cash flows

Budgets

Forecasts, etc.

Any job involving the use of numbers can be done on a spreadsheet.

The biggest advantage that a spreadsheet has over other methods of manipulating data - using a table in a word processing application for example, is its ability to constantly update figures without the user having to do any calculations. Once a spreadsheet is set up correctly, its calculations will always be correct and any changes in data are recalculated automatically.

Spreadsheets can also take basic data and present it in an attractive ways, for example as formatted lists, tables and graphs.

Exercise 2 - Starting the Program

Guidelines:

There are numerous ways to start *Excel*. The following method is recommended for beginners. When the computer is started, the *Windows* desktop will automatically be shown.

Actions:

1. Click once on 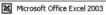 to show the list of options available. All *Windows* applications can be started from here.

2. Place the mouse cursor over **All Programs** (this is **Programs** in earlier versions of *Windows*), then **Microsoft Office** and then click
🗷 Microsoft Office Excel 2003

Note: Your PC may have Excel grouped under a different name or not grouped at all. If this is the case, select the relevant group name and then click
🗷 Microsoft Office Excel 2003

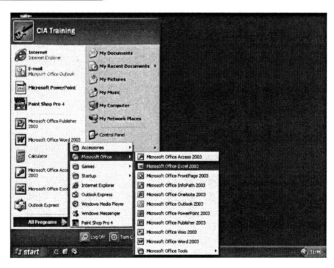

*Note: The listing under **All Programs** and the applications listed at the left of the **Start** menu, will be different depending on the software that is installed on the PC and which applications have been used recently.*

Exercise 3 - The Layout of the Excel Screen

Guidelines:

The main area of the *Excel* screen is the **Worksheet Area**. This is a grid where the data is shown and manipulated.

The top line is called the **Title Bar** and shows the current workbook in use (**Book1**) and the application (*Microsoft Excel*). Below that there is a **Menu Bar**, where commands are selected using the mouse. Below the **Menu Bar** is another bar, known as the **Toolbar**. This bar contains buttons that are used to quickly access the most commonly used menu commands. At the bottom of the screen is a grey bar called the **Status Bar**, where information is displayed on the current task. Under that is the **Taskbar** which displays icons that represent workbooks that are currently open.

At the right of the screen is an area called the **Task Pane**, which helps to perform common tasks. It can be changed depending on the task currently being performed. Various types of **Task Pane** are available.

Note: *If the* **Task Pane** *is not visible, select* **View | Task Pane**.

Actions:

1. The **Office Assistant** may be visible. Click on it with the right mouse button and select **Hide** to remove it from the screen. The **Office Assistant** is part of *Excel's* **Help** facility but it is not covered in this guide.

Note: *Some of the buttons may be different, because Excel automatically customises the toolbars and menu lists to reflect the options selected most often. See the following exercises for more information.*

Exercise 4 - The Menu Bar

Guidelines:

The **Menu Bar** contains all of the commands needed to use *Excel*, within drop down lists. The most recently used commands from a menu are included in a shortened list, which is shown first when the menu is selected. The remaining, missing commands can be revealed at any time. If a command is not used for some time, it may be replaced on the short, personalised menu by a command that has been used more recently.

Note: *This customisation feature may cause the menus to look slightly different to those in this guide, but the principles remain the same.*

Actions:

1. Look below the **Title Bar**, to see the **Menu Bar**, where drop down menus are selected and commands chosen using the mouse.

2. Double click on **Edit**. This displays the full **Edit Menu**.

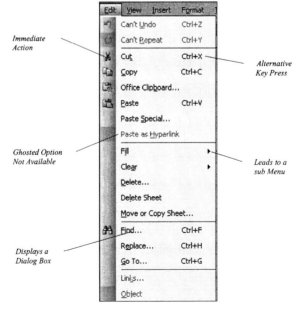

Immediate Action

Alternative Key Press

Ghosted Option Not Available

Leads to a sub Menu

Displays a Dialog Box

continued over

Exercise 4 - Continued

3. Click again on the same menu name or press <**Esc**> twice to remove the menu.

4. Single click on **Edit**, the menu appears, showing a reduced choice of commands.

5. Chevrons 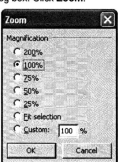 appear at the bottom of the list for a few seconds. If they are clicked on, the menu will expand. Click on **Edit** to close the menu.

6. To use the chevrons, click on **Edit** and immediately click on the chevrons at the bottom of the list to expand it to display the entire **Edit** menu.

7. Notice how some options are **ghosted** (pale grey). This means that they are not available at present.

8. Position the mouse pointer over **View** to display the **View** menu. Options with three dots after the command lead to a dialog box. Click **Zoom**.

9. This dialog box allows the display to be enlarged or reduced. Click **Cancel** to close the dialog box.

10. Click the **Edit** menu and look at the commands that have a black triangle after them. These commands lead to a sub menu. Move the pointer over **Clear**.

continued over

Exercise 4 - Continued

11.　Another list is displayed, with four options.

12.　Options not followed by three dots or a black triangle like **Cut** and **Copy**, would perform the command directly if clicked. Options followed by a key press combination, e.g. **Ctrl+C**, can be executed at any time by pressing the specified keys. Click **Edit** to close the menu.

13.　These descriptions of menu commands apply to all menus. Double click on the **File** menu to view the full range of options. Notice which commands lead to dialog boxes, lists, direct action and those which are not available at present. Place the mouse pointer over each of the other menus in turn to do the same.

14.　Close the open menu with a single click.

Exercise 5 - Toolbars

Guidelines:

Toolbars allow quick access to the most commonly used commands, each is represented by a button. To save space on the screen many buttons are hidden, but they can easily be displayed. The toolbars become personalised after being used, a button replaces another on the toolbar, which is then hidden.

Note: Toolbars may not look exactly as shown in this guide, because they can be customised by the user, but the principles remain the same.

Actions:

1.　The **Toolbar** is just beneath the **Menu Bar**. Move the mouse pointer over a button on the **Toolbar** and leave it there for a few seconds.

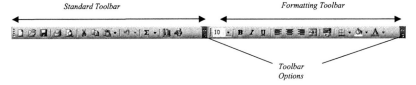

Standard Toolbar　　　　　　　*Formatting Toolbar*

Toolbar Options

Note: These toolbars may be beneath one another.

continued over

Exercise 5 - Continued

2.   A **ToolTip** appears, 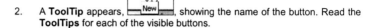, showing the name of the button. Read the **ToolTips** for each of the visible buttons.

3.   Chevrons, ▓, on the **Toolbar Options** indicate that more buttons are available. If chevrons are visible click on them at the right of the **Standard Toolbar**. Now all of the buttons from both the Toolbars are available.

4.   Move the mouse pointer over | Add or Remove Buttons ▾ |, then formatting, | Formatting ▸ |, to see all of the other buttons which are available to be added.

5.   A list of the possible buttons appears; those with ticks are on the main toolbar, either visible or hidden.

6.   Click on the worksheet to close the menu.

7.   Toolbars can be moved so that more buttons can be seen. To see both the **Standard** and the **Formatting** toolbars at the same time, click on the **Toolbar Options** for either Toolbar and select **Show Buttons on Two Rows**.

8.   To replace both the toolbars on one row, click on the **Toolbar Options** for either Toolbar and select **Show Buttons on One Row**.

9.   Move the mouse pointer over the vertical line of dots, ▓, between the Toolbars, until it changes to a four headed arrow, as in the diagram below:

10. Click and hold down the mouse, then drag it carefully from side to side so that it alters the relative size of each Toolbar.

11. Drag the vertical line of dots so that each Toolbar occupies about half the screen width.

12. Select **View | Toolbars** to see the toolbars currently available. The toolbars currently in use have a tick next to them.

13. Any listed toolbar can be added to the screen by clicking on it. Click on the **Picture** toolbar and it appears on the screen.

14. To remove the **Picture** toolbar from the screen, select **View | Toolbars** and click on **Picture** again.

Exercise 6 - The Worksheet Window

Guidelines:

Information is stored in **Workbooks**. Each workbook contains 3 **worksheets** by default. Workbooks can contain up to 255 worksheets. Each worksheet has 256 columns and 65,536 rows. The columns are referred to by letters, **A, B, C,** ...**AA, AB**... **IV** and the rows are referred to by numbers **1, 2, 3,** ...**65536**.

These letters and numbers are shown in the **Row** and **Column** borders on the worksheet. The point where a column and row intersect is known as a **Cell**. Each cell is identified by the column letter and row number, which forms the intersection, e.g. the cell formed by the intersection of column D and row 7 is known as cell **D7**. The letter and number of the currently selected cell is called the **Active Cell Reference**.

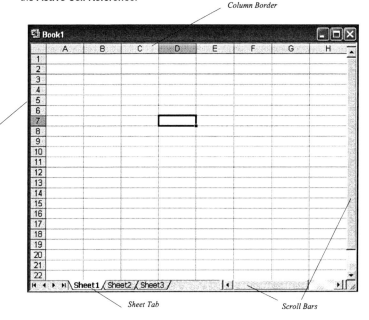

Column Border

Row Border

Sheet Tab

Scroll Bars

There are **Scroll Bars** at the right and bottom edges of the worksheet, which are used to show different areas of the worksheet.

Each worksheet in the workbook has a name (at the moment they are named Sheet1, Sheet2, Sheet3) and each has a **Sheet Tab**. They are shown at the bottom of the window. When more sheets are added, more buttons are added.

Exercise 7 - Closing Excel

Guidelines:

> When *Excel* is closed, if any workbooks are still open and have not been saved, a warning will be displayed with an option to save the changes.

Actions:

1. Select the **File** menu to display the drop down menu.

2. Place the mouse pointer over **Exit** and click once.

*Note: Excel can also be closed by clicking the **Close** button, 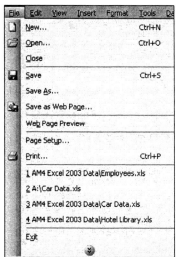, in the top right corner of the screen.*

3. Select **No** if there is a prompt to save.

Exercise 8 - Revision

Note: The answers for this exercise are listed on page 73.

1. Start *Excel*.

2. What is the name of the current workbook?

3. List the menu names in order from left to right.

4. Click on the **View** menu, and notice which toolbars are currently in use.

5. Position the cursor over the icon on the toolbar. What is the tooltip?

6. Close *Excel*.

Section 2

Open, Save and Close Workbooks

By the end of this Section you should be able to:

Open an Existing Workbook
Move Around Using the Keyboard
Save an Existing Workbook
Close a Workbook

Exercise 9 - Opening a Workbook

Guidelines:

Workbooks saved to disk are only useful if they can be opened to use again.

Actions:

1.   Open *Excel*.

2.   Click **More** under **Open** in the **Getting Started Task Pane** to display the **Open** dialog box.

*Note: The **Open** dialog box can also be displayed by clicking the **Open** button,*  , *on the **Toolbar** or selecting **File | Open** from the **Menu Bar**.*

3.   From the **Look in** box, select the location where the data files are stored.

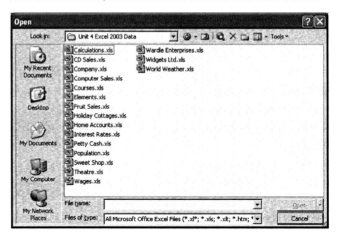

4.   In the list of files, click on **Petty Cash**. This is the workbook, which is to be opened. Click the **Open** button, [**Open**   ▼].

Note: Double clicking on its name in the list will also open the workbook directly.

5.   This is a simple spreadsheet showing a running total of petty cash as expenses are deducted.

6.   Leave the workbook open for the next exercise.

Exercise 10 - Moving Around using the Keyboard

Guidelines:

The keyboard or the mouse can be used to move around the screen. This guide will use only a few of the available key presses, as shown below.

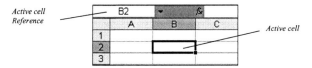

Active cell Reference

Active cell

The **Current** or **Active cell** is shown on the screen by a dark border. The **Active Cell Reference** is shown in the **Formula Bar**. The active cell can be moved around the worksheet using various key presses. The keys are:

→	-	Moves one cell to the right
←	-	Moves one cell to the left
↓	-	Moves down one cell
↑	-	Moves up one cell
\<Home\>	-	Moves to column A
\<Ctrl Home\>	-	Moves directly to cell A1

Actions:

1. Open the workbook **Petty Cash** if not already open. The **Active Cell** should be **A1**, if not, click in it. This should appear at the left of the **Formula Bar**. Press each of the following keys once →, ↓, ←, ↑, observing their effect on the current cell and the cell reference in the **Formula Bar**. You should end up back in cell **A1**.

2. Click the mouse in cell **D10.** Press **\<Ctrl Home\>** to jump directly back to cell **A1**.

3. Click in cell **E14** Press **\<Home\>** to return to column **A**.

4. Press **\<Ctrl Home\>** to return to cell **A1**.

5. Leave the workbook open for the next exercise.

Exercise 11 - Closing a Workbook

Guidelines:

It is possible to have more than one workbook open at a time. Usually, however, the current workbook is removed before opening a new one.

When closing a workbook, a warning dialog box will be displayed if any changes have been made to the current workbook since it was last saved.

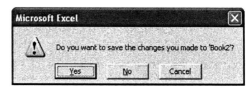

The user will be asked "Do you want to save changes you made to ..." and the options **Yes, No** and **Cancel** will be displayed. Selecting **Yes** will save the file under its original name before closing, **No** will close the file without saving and **Cancel** will return to the worksheet.

Actions:

1. Use **Petty Cash** from the previous exercise.

2. Select **File | Close** to close the workbook. In this instance, no changes have been made to the workbook since it was last saved, so it will close without displaying the **Save Changes** dialog box (if the dialog box does appear, click **No**).

*Note: The **Close Window** button,* ☒ *, can be used to close a workbook. Be careful not to close Excel.*

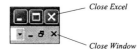

Close Excel

Close Window

Exercise 12 - Saving a Named Workbook

Guidelines:

There are two commands used when saving a workbook: **Save** and **Save As**. **Save** saves the file under the same name as previously used and overwrites any older version without prompting. If a file is to be saved under a different name, or in a different location, keeping the old version intact, then use **Save As**.

Actions:

1. Open the file **CD Sales**.

	A	B	C	D	E	F
1						
2		*CD Sales Ltd.*				
3						
4						
5		Quarters	First	Second	Third	Fourth
6		Sales	405	397	376	527
7		Turnover	£4,050	£3,970	£3,760	£5,270
8		Profit	£1,012.50	£992.50	£940.00	£1,317.50
9						

2. Click the **Save** button, 🖫, on the toolbar. The current version of the workbook is immediately saved, overwriting the original version.

*Note: The menu selection **File | Save** is an alternative to using the **Save** button.*

3. To save the workbook with a different name, select **File | Save As** to display the **Save As** dialog box.

4. Type **CD Sales2** in the **File name** box to save the file with this name (the original name can be edited by clicking on it and then making the change).

5. Check that the current folder is correct in the **Save in** box. Click the **Save** button, [Save], in the dialog box. The current version of the workbook is saved as a new file and the original workbook is unaffected.

6. Close the workbook.

7. Click **Open**, 📂 and look at the available files. Both the original **CD Sales** file and the new **CD Sales2** file now exist in the folder.

continued over

Exercise 12 - Continued

8.   Select **CD Sales2** and click the open button, Open ▾.

9.   **Save As** will not overwrite an existing file without warning. Select **File | Save As** and save the workbook again as **CD Sales2**. Click the **Save** button, Save. The following message is displayed.

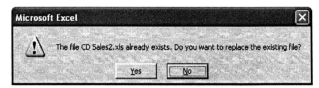

10. Click **Yes** to replace the existing file.

11. Close the workbook.

Exercise 13 - Revision

Note: The answers for this exercise are listed on page 73.

1. Open the workbook **Holiday Cottages**.

2. Using the mouse, select the cell **H9**. What is the value in that cell?

3. Use the arrow keys to move two cells down. What is the new **Active Cell Reference** and the value contained in the active cell.

4. Use the **Save** button to save the workbook.

5. Use **Save As** to save another copy of the workbook in a file called **Holiday Cottages 2002**.

6. Close the workbook.

7. Select **File | Open** and look at the list of files. How many now refer to Holiday Cottages?

8. Click **Cancel** to close the **Open** dialog box.

Exercise 14 - Revision

1. Open the workbook **Theatre**.

2. Do not close the workbook, but open the second workbook **Interest Rates**.

3. Select **File | Close** to close **Interest Rates**.

4. Use the **Close Window** button to close **Theatre**.

5. Close *Excel* using any method.

6. Start *Excel* again.

Section 3

Creating a Worksheet

By the end of this Section you should be able to:

Understand Spreadsheet Structure
Enter Labels
Enter Numbers
Save a New Workbook

Exercise 15 - Spreadsheet Structure

Guidelines:

A spreadsheet model is a block of occupied cells.

Cells within an *Excel* worksheet can contain either **Text** (Labels), **Numbers** (Values) or **Formulas** (calculations, involving contents of other cells). **Labels** are normally used for describing the contents of the worksheet, as column or row titles for example, whereas **Values** are used for calculations.

A typical model has no blank rows or columns within it, the relationship between **Text**, **Numbers** and **Formulas** is shown below (remember this is a typical example - cell contents can be arranged in any way).

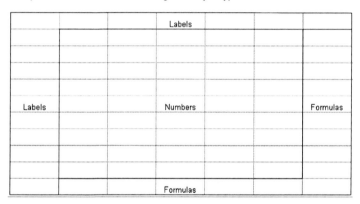

Spreadsheet shape is important when printing. Create spreadsheets so that they are either long and thin or short and fat, so that they can be paged in one direction.

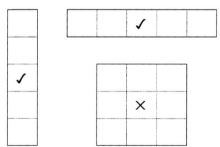

Exercise 16 - Creating a Spreadsheet

Guidelines:

Workbooks can contain many sheets. When creating a spreadsheet model, start on **Sheet1** (the default) and begin by using the top left corner. Normally a **Title** is entered in cell **A1** and the main block starts in either **A2** or **A3**.

Entering information into a cell

To enter information into a cell, either click on the cell, or use the cursor movement keys to place the **Active Cell** in the correct position and start typing. When entering information the text appears in the **Formula Bar** as well as in the cell.

To complete an entry either use **<Enter>**, the cursor movement keys (arrow keys), click on the **Enter** box in the **Formula Bar**:

or click on another cell. When **<Enter>** is used, the default action is for the active cell to move down to the cell below, whereas the arrow keys allow movement in any direction, ready for the next entry.

Either the keyboard or the mouse can be used to move around, but the keyboard is used to input (type in) data. This is why it is sometimes referred to as an **input device**.

Labels

Labels are entered as text and are usually placed down column **A** and across row **2** or **3** from column **B**. Text is aligned to the left by default (placed at the left edge of the cell). If the text entered does not fit, then the size of the text or the size of the cell can be changed.

Numbers

Select the cell, type the number and complete the entry with any of the methods described above. Numbers are right aligned by default (placed flush to the right edge of the cell).

Note: To display numbers with leading zeros, start the entry with an apostrophe, e.g. '0786. The entry is now treated as text but calculations can still be performed on it without modification. Trailing zeros in decimals are displayed using formatting.

Exercise 17 - Starting a New Workbook

Guidelines:

A blank workbook must be started to begin creating a new spreadsheet.

Actions:

1.   Close any open workbooks.

2.   Start a new workbook by selecting **File | New**.

3.   This displays the **New Workbook Task Pane** dialog box allowing templates to be selected, if required. Templates can be found under **Templates**. There are other options, but these differ depending on what has been installed. Under **New** select **Blank workbook**.

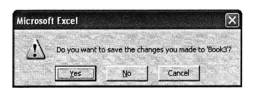

4.   Close the current workbook using the **Close Window** button, ☒.

5.   A new workbook can also be started by clicking the **New** button, ☐. Click the button to open a workbook using the current default settings.

6.   Type your name in cell **A1**. Press **<Enter>**.

7.   Close the workbook using any method. A message box is displayed.

![Microsoft Excel message box: Do you want to save the changes you made to 'Book3'? Yes / No / Cancel]

8.   Click **No** to close the workbook without saving.

Exercise 18 - Entering Labels

Guidelines:

Labels are normally used for describing the contents of the worksheet, as column or row titles for example.

Actions:

1. Open a new workbook, as in the previous exercise. Cell **A1** should be active (a heavy border). If not, click on it.

2. A label is entered into a particular cell by typing. In cell **A1**, type **Computer Equipment Sales** (when entering information into a cell, notice that the text appears in the **Formula Bar** as well as in the cell).

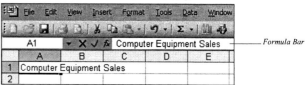

Formula Bar

3. To complete a cell entry press **<Enter>**. The active cell moves down to cell **A2**. Even though the long title is stored completely in cell **A1**, it is displayed on the worksheet flowing into cells **B1** and **C1**, but this is only because currently those cells are not being used.

Note: Selecting **Tools | Options | Edit** *allows a choice of where the next entry will be placed after* **<Enter>** *is pressed. Any direction may be selected under* **Move selection after Enter**. *If repeated data entry is along a row or down a column, use this option to determine the direction after pressing* **<Enter>**.

4. Move to cell **A3** and type **Sales**. Place the text in **A3** by pressing →. This automatically enters the data into **A3** and moves the cursor to the right, ready for the next entry.

5. Complete the table by entering the data as below. Do not try to correct any errors that may be made.

	A	B	C	D	E	F
1	Computer Equipment Sales					
2						
3	Sales	PCs	Printers	Scanners	Total Units	
4	John					
5	Natalie					
6	Asif					
7	Total					
8						

6. Leave the workbook open for the next exercise.

Exercise 19 - Entering Numbers

Guidelines:

Numbers must begin with one of the following characters: **0 1 2 3 4 5 6 7 8 9 . + -** or the currency symbol **£**. It is very important to enter numbers accurately so you don't produce calculations that produce incorrect answers.

Actions:

1.   Move to **B4**. Type **9**. Enter the rest of the information below into the correct cells.

	A	B	C	D	E	F
1	Computer Equipment Sales					
2						
3	Sales	PCs	Printers	Scanners	Total Units	
4	John	9	3	2		
5	Natalie	5	5	4		
6	Asif	7	2	5		
7	Total					
8						

2.   Do **NOT** close the workbook. Leave it open for the next exercise.

Note: Remember that all values are moved automatically to the right edge of the column and the labels to the left.

Exercise 20 - Saving a New Workbook

Guidelines:

After creating worksheets, they need to be saved as a workbook so they can be used again.

The **Save As** process includes selecting a location to save to and giving the workbook a name.

Actions:

1. Select **File | Save As** to display the **Save As** dialog box.

2. Workbooks are saved by default to the **My Documents** folder on the hard drive. Select the location where the data files are stored from the drop down **Save in** box.

3. The default workbook name **Book#** (where **#** is a number) is in the **File name** box. Type **Equipment Sales** as the new file name to replace the default name.

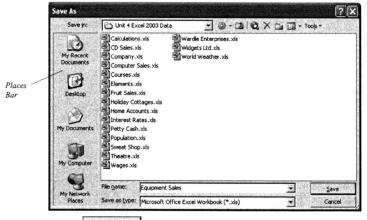

4. Click the [**Save**] button to save the file.

5. The workbook will be saved as **Equipment Sales** (a file extension **.xls** is added automatically, although sometimes not displayed). The **Title Bar** changes to show the new filename, **Equipment Sales**.

Note: When saving an unnamed workbook, either select File | Save As, File | Save or use Save button, on the toolbar. All these commands display Save As dialog box.

6. Close the workbook.

Exercise 21 - Revision

1. Start a new workbook and create the following worksheet. To move in the correct direction, use the arrow keys to complete an entry. Enter your name in place of **Fred Bloggs**.

	A	B	C	D	E	F
1	Fred Bloggs					
2						
3	Number	Add	Subtract	Multiply	Divide	
4	First	6	7	3	12	
5	Second	3	4	5	4	
6	Result					
7						

2. This worksheet is used as part of a later exercise. Save the workbook as **Formulas**, in the same location as the other data files used in the guide.

3. Close the workbook.

Exercise 22 - Revision

1. Start a new workbook and create a worksheet as below.

	A	B	C	D	E
1					
2					
3	Fruit	Apples	Pears	Oranges	Total
4	Jan	36	38	26	
5	Feb	40	26	37	
6	Mar	53	23	84	
7	Total				
8					

2. Save the workbook as **Fruit**.

3. Close the workbook.

Exercise 23 - Revision

1.   Open the workbook **Sweet Shop**.

2.   In cell **A4** enter **Mars Bars**.

3.   In **A5** enter **Milky Ways** and in **A6** enter **Kit Kats**.

4.   The **Price** for each item is **50p**, **35p** and **37p** respectively. Enter the numbers in the format **0.50**, etc.

5.   The numbers sold were **3**, **4** and **2**. Enter this information into the worksheet.

6.   Save the workbook as **Chocolate**.

7.   Enter your name in cell **A1**.

8.   Close the workbook using the **Close** button (click **Yes** when the program asks whether to save).

Section 4

Formulas

By the end of this Section you should be able to:

Create Simple Formulas
Understand Mathematical Operators
Use Brackets
Understand Relative Addressing
Select Cells with the Mouse to Create Formulas
Use AutoSum
Copy Formulas

Exercise 24 - Introducing Formulas

Guidelines:

A calculation in *Excel* is called a **Formula**. Formulas are used to calculate answers from numbers entered on the sheet, e.g. sales for the year, net profit in a month, overall profitability of the company, etc.

All formulas begin with an equals sign (=), followed by the calculation.

Formulas automatically calculate results from the data. Any changes in the data will cause the formulas to be recalculated automatically.

Actions:

1. Open the workbook **Formulas**, created in Exercise 21. If you did not complete Exercise 21, create a new worksheet as shown below (leave cell **B6** empty for now) and then save it as **Formulas**.

2. To add the contents of **B4** and **B5**, make **B6** the active cell by clicking on it.

3. Do not add spaces and use the **+** symbol on the numeric keypad at the right of the keyboard to type in **=b4+b5 <Enter>**. The cells being selected in the formula are highlighted automatically when entered on the screen. This creates a formula to add the contents of cells **B4** and **B5**.

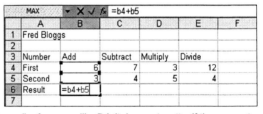

MAX		▼ X √ ƒₓ =b4+b5			
A	**B**	**C**	**D**	**E**	**F**
1	Fred Bloggs				
2					
3	Number	Add	Subtract	Multiply	Divide
4	First	6	7	3	12
5	Second	3	4	5	4
6	Result	=b4+b5			
7					

*Note: When entering cell references, like **B4**, it does not matter if they are entered in capitals or not, as Excel converts them to uppercase.*

4. Click back on cell **B6** and note the cell displays **9** and the **Formula Bar** displays **=B4+B5**, the formula.

B6		▼ ƒₓ =B4+B5			
A	**B**	**C**	**D**	**E**	**F**
1	Fred Bloggs				
2					
3	Number	Add	Subtract	Multiply	Divide
4	First	6	7	3	12
5	Second	3	4	5	4
6	Result	9			
7					

5. Leave the workbook **Formulas** open.

Exercise 25 - Mathematical Operators

Guidelines:

The basic mathematical operators are add, subtract, multiply and divide. You have already used the operator **+**; the others are introduced here. The symbols on a keyboard are slightly different to those used normally and are:

+　Add
-　Subtract
*　Multiply
/　Divide

These symbols appear twice, one set placed around the main keyboard and the other set on the numeric keypad (right side). The keypad is easier to use because the keys are closer together and the <**Shift**> key is not used.

Other mathematical operations are used via **Functions** These are not covered in this guide.

Actions:

1.　With the workbook **Formulas** open, click on cell **C6**.

Note: *To use the numeric keypad for number entries, the **Num Lock** light on the keyboard must be on. If not, press <**Num Lock**>.*

2.　Enter the formula to subtract the two numbers above **=c4-c5**. Complete the entry by pressing the right arrow key. The answer is displayed as **3**.

3.　In cell **D6**, enter the formula to multiply the two numbers above **=d4*d5**. Complete the entry by pressing the right arrow key. The answer is displayed as **15**.

4.　In cell **E6**, enter the formula to divide the two numbers above **=e4/e5**. Complete the entry by pressing the right arrow key. The answer is displayed as **3**.

F6	▼	*fx*				
	A	B	C	D	E	F	G
1	Fred Bloggs						
2							
3	Number	Add	Subtract	Multiply	Divide		
4	First	6	7	3	12		
5	Second	3	4	5	4		
6	Result	9	3	15	3		
7							

5.　Leave the workbook open for the next exercise.

Exercise 26 - Brackets

Guidelines:

When more than one operator is used in one formula, then the order becomes important, e.g. **D23+E17/E19**. *Excel* performs calculations in this order: **Brackets** over **Division**, **Multiplication**, **Addition** and finally **Subtraction** (the **BODMAS** theory). Brackets are added to force *Excel* to perform calculations in a different order to normal, i.e. calculations within brackets are done first.

Actions:

1. Open **Formulas** if not already open from previous exercise. Click on cell **C10** and enter the label **Item 1**.

2. Enter the labels in cells **B11** to **B14** below. Enter the numbers in cells **C11** to **C13** below.

	A	B	C	D	E	F
1	Fred Bloggs					
2						
3	Number	Add	Subtract	Multiply	Divide	
4	First	6	7	3	12	
5	Second	3	4	5	4	
6	Result	9	3	15	3	
7						
8						
9						
10			Item 1			
11		Sell Price	10			
12		Buy Price	6			
13		Sold	3			
14		Profit				
15						

3. To calculate the profit, click on cell **C14** and type the formula **=c11-c12*c13**.

4. Press **<Enter>** to complete the formula. The answer given is **-8** (this is because the multiplication is carried out before the subtraction: the **BODMAS** theory).

5. Click on cell **C14** and this time add brackets around the subtraction (the old formula is replaced by the new). Type **=(c11-c12)*c13 <Enter>**.

6. Check that the answer displayed is now **12**. Profit per item **10-6**, which is **4** multiplied by the number sold, **3**, giving the total profit of **12**. The answer is now correct.

7. Leave the workbook open for the next exercise.

Exercise 27 - Selecting Cells with the Mouse

Guidelines:

When entering formulas that involve the use of cell references, e.g. **=E6+F6** typing errors can be made. The mouse can be used to enter the cell references. This is also called **Pointing**.

The mouse pointer is moved to the required cell and clicked.

Actions:

1. If the workbook **Formulas** is not open then open it.

2. Move to cell **D10** and add another label **Item 2**.

3. In **D11** add another **Sell Price** of 8.

4. In cell **D12** enter a **Buy Price** of **5,** and in cell **D13** enter the number **Sold** as **10**.

5. In cell **D14** enter the formula to calculate the **Profit**, using the mouse to enter the cell references. Type =(to start the formula and instead of typing **d11**, point and click on **D11** with the mouse.

	A	B	C	D	E	F
1	Fred Bloggs					
2						
3	Number	Add	Subtract	Multiply	Divide	
4	First	6	7	3	12	
5	Second	3	4	5	4	
6	Result		9	3	15	3
7						
8						
9						
10			Item 1	Item 2		
11		Sell Price	10	8		
12		Buy Price	6	5		
13		Sold	3	10		
14		Profit	12	=(D11		
15						

6. Press the **-** key, then click on cell **D12**. Press **)** then * followed by a click on cell **D13** and then press **<Enter>**. The cell will display the result, **30**.

D14	▼		*fx*	=(D11-D12)*D13	
	A	B	C	D	E
9					
10			Item 1	Item 2	
11		Sell Price	10	8	
12		Buy Price	6	5	
13		Sold	3	10	
14		Profit	12	30	
15					

*The **Formula Bar** shows the formula and the cell shows the answer*

7. Save the workbook using the same filename, **Formulas**, then close it.

Exercise 28 - AutoSum

Guidelines:

The most common formula is addition. This calculation has been simplified by the creation of a **Function** called **Sum**. Functions (covered in the CLAIT Plus guide) are pre-calculated formulas. There is a button on the toolbar called **AutoSum** that creates the **Sum** function automatically.

Actions:

1. Open the workbook **Equipment Sales** created earlier, or the supplied workbook **Computer Sales**.

2. Click in cell **B7** The three cells above need to be added together to find the total. Add them using the mouse to select each of the cells. The formula is **=B4+B5+B6**. The answer should be **21**.

3. As more and more numbers are added this method becomes unworkable. There is a function: **SUM** that adds a group of cells. This is so widely used that there is a button on the toolbar to perform it automatically.

4. Select cell **C7** and click on the **AutoSum** button, [Σ ▾] (if this is not displayed then click [▪] to display more buttons).

	A	B	C	D	E	F
1	Computer Equipment Sales					
2						
3	Sales	PC's	Printers	Scanners	Total Units	
4	John	9	3	2		
5	Natalie	5	5	4		
6	Asif	7	2	5		
7	Total	21	=SUM(C4:C6)			
8			SUM(**number1**, [number2], ...)			
9						

5. The program looks for numbers to add. **AutoSum** tries above first, if there are no numbers above it looks left. **AutoSum** finds the 3 numbers and adds them. Press <**Enter**> to complete the function and display the answer **10** in cell **C7**.

6. Click in cell **E4** and click the **AutoSum** button, [Σ ▾], which is now displayed on the toolbar. There are no numbers above so **AutoSum** looks left and sums the 3 cells **B4**, **C4** and **D4**. Press <**Enter**>. The answer is **14**.

Note: *AutoSum only works without any help when numbers have already been entered into the worksheet. If AutoSum has numbers in both directions it will sum upwards by default.*

7. The other formulas are created later by copying. Close the workbook and select **Yes** to save the changes, using the same workbook name.

Exercise 29 - Using the Fill Handle to Copy

Guidelines:

Ranges can be quickly filled with data by using the **Fill Handle**, at the bottom right corner of the active cell.

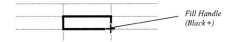

It is only possible to drag in one direction, i.e. along a row or down a column.

An extra feature of dragging the **Fill Handle** is the ability to automatically fill ranges with titles such as months of the year, days of the week, any text ending with a number and dates.

Actions:

1. On a new worksheet enter your first name in **B2**.

2. Select **B2** and move the mouse pointer to the **Fill Handle** of **B2**. Click and hold down the mouse button, then drag the mouse to the right along the row of cells to **G2**.

3. In **E4** enter **63**. Click and drag the **Fill Handle** of **E4** down to **E7**. The entry **63** is repeated.

4. Click the cell **E4**. Hold <**Ctrl**> while dragging the **Fill Handle** to cell **I4**.

	63			
63			67	
63				
63				

A ToolTip shows the extent of the range as a caption.

5. Release the mouse button, before releasing <**Ctrl**>. Holding **Ctrl** while dragging has caused the range to be filled with a series of numbers rather than the same number repeated. This method is very useful for quickly numbering cells, especially rows.

Note: *Whenever using the **Fill Handle**, with or without the **Ctrl** key, a **Smart Tag** is displayed at the end of the new range. Clicking on the Smart Tag will display options to either **Copy Cells** or **Fill Series** the range and this can be used to override the default action. The ToolTip for the Smart Tag is **Auto Fill Options**.*

6. Close the workbook without saving.

© CiA Training Ltd 2004

Exercise 30 - Copying Formulas

Guidelines:

The copying of formulas can be carried out in precisely the same way as labels. If the user wishes to use the same formula in another position, e.g. to total the next column of figures, then the references of the columns within the formula will require adjustment.

By default *Excel* will carry out this adjustment automatically. This is because cell addresses are held as **Relative Addresses** (this is covered in the next exercise).

Actions:

1. Open the workbook used in Exercise 28 (either **Equipment Sales** or **Computer Sales**).

		Labels		
				Formula
Labels		Numbers		
	Formula			

*Note: When creating a typical **Spreadsheet Model**, only the formulas to the right of the first row and at the bottom of the first column are created. The **Fill Handle** is then used to copy each of the formulas to adjacent cells (the grand total, bottom right, can be either the sum of the rows or of the columns).*

2. Select cell **C7**. Notice the formula bar shows the calculation was made using **=SUM(C4:C6)**. This formula is to be copied to cell **D7**.

3. Click and drag the fill handle of cell **C7** to **D7**.

continued over

Exercise 30 - Continued

	A	B	C	D	E	F
1	Computer Equipment Sales					
2						
3	Sales	PC's	Printers	Scanners	Total Units	
4	John	9	3	2		
5	Natalie	5	5	4		
6	Asif	7	2	5		
7	Total	21	10	11		
8						
9						

4.   Examine the formula in **D7**. It now shows **=SUM(D4:D6)**.

*Note: The **Smart Tag** for the copy action is shown to the right of cell **D7**.*

5.   The formula in **E4** is to be copied using the same process to **E5**, **E6** and **E7**.   Click and drag the fill handle from **E4** to **E7**.   The completed spreadsheet should now appear as below.

	A	B	C	D	E	F
1	Computer Equipment Sales					
2						
3	Sales	PC's	Printers	Scanners	Total Units	
4	John	9	3	2	14	
5	Natalie	5	5	4	14	
6	Asif	7	2	5	14	
7	Total	21	10	11	42	
8						
9						

6.   Save the workbook using the name **Results** and then close it.

Exercise 31 - Relative Addressing

Guidelines:

As a formula is copied across a range of cells, the formulas change automatically. The calculation is performed on cells in the positions relative to those copied, e.g. **B2+B3** becomes **C2+C3** then **D2+D3**, as the formula is copied from column **B** to column **C** to column **D**.

The formulas can be copied to any cells in any position on a worksheet.

Actions:

1. Start a new workbook.

2. In cell **B2** enter **7** and in **B3** enter **8**. In cell **B4** create a formula **=B2+B3** to add the two numbers.

3. Click on cell **B4** and click the **Copy** button, [icon]. Move to cell **D8** and click **Paste** button, [icon], to copy the formula.

Note: A Paste Options Smart Tag is displayed after each paste action. This allows formatting options to be specified.

4. The formula is copied and adds the cells relative to the formula, i.e. the two cells directly above, which are empty at present. Enter **5** and **3** into cells **D6** and **D7**.

D8			=D6+D7	
	A	B	C	D	E
1					
2		7			
3		8			
4		15			
5					
6				5	
7				3	
8				8	
9					

Note: All formulas copied are relative whether using Copy or the Fill Handle.

5. Click on cell **B4** and drag its **Fill Handle** across three columns. The results are displayed as **0,** because there is no data above the formulas yet.

6. Examine the formulas in cells **C4**, **D4** and **E4**.

7. Enter numbers into the two cells above the three formulas to test and see if they work.

8. Close the workbook <u>without</u> saving.

Exercise 32 - Revision

Note: The answers for this exercise are listed on page 73.

1. Open the file **Fruit** created in Exercise 21. If you did not complete Exercise 21, create a new workbook as below and save it as **Fruit**.

2. This is a worksheet produced by a person who sells a limited number of fruits from a barrow in the High Street. The numbers are boxes of fruit sold per month.

	A	B	C	D	E
1					
2					
3	Fruit	Apples	Pears	Oranges	Total
4	Jan	36	38	26	
5	Feb	40	26	37	
6	Mar	53	23	84	
7	Total				
8					

3. Use the **AutoSum** button to calculate the total boxes of **Apples** sold in cell **B7**.

4. Calculate the total boxes of fruit sold during **January** in cell **E4**.

5. Find out how many boxes of fruit were sold in **February** and **March** by completing cells **E5**, and **E6** using the **Fill Handle**.

6. Similarly, copy the formula from **B7** to **C7, D7** and finally **E7**.

7. How many boxes of fruit were sold in the first three months of the year?

8. Save the file as **Fruit2** and close the worksheet.

Exercise 33 - Revision

Note: The answers for this exercise are listed on page 73.

1. Open the workbook **Population**. This workbook lists all the major countries of the world showing their land size and population.

2. You are required to sum each of the four main regions of the world. Sum the population of **Europe** in cell **D22** (the range **D4:D21**) using **AutoSum**.

3. Sum the other three regions: **Asia** in cell **D38**, **America** in cell **D52** and **Australasia** in cell **D60**.

4. Type your name in cell **A1**.

5. Save the workbook as **Population2** and then close it.

Section 5

Editing Cells

By the end of this Section you should be able to:

Edit Cells by Overtyping
Delete Cell Contents
Edit Data in the Formula Bar
Edit Data in a Cell

Exercise 34 - Overtyping

Guidelines:

If the cell entry is short, then the simplest way to edit is to click on the cell and enter the new data. This overwrites the previous entry.

Actions:

1. Start a new workbook and type **Fred** into cell **B7** and press **<Enter>**.

2. Make **B7** the active cell, type your first name and press **<Enter>** to replace **Fred** with your name. The contents of any cell can be overwritten in this way.

3. Click on cell **B7**. Type **HELLO**, but BEFORE pressing **<Enter>** press **<Esc>**, the **Escape** key. This cancels the new input and leaves the cell contents unchanged.

4. In the current cell type **HELLO** again, but before pressing **<Enter>** click on

    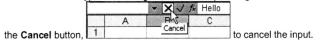

    the **Cancel** button, to cancel the input.

5. Close the worksheet without saving.

6. Open the workbook **Courses**. This shows the attendance on four courses over three terms.

7. In cell **B4**, overtype the data by typing **12** and press **<Enter>**.

8. Notice that the calculated totals are automatically updated as soon as this value is altered. Total attendance for Spanish goes to **29**, total attendance for Term1 is now **41** and the total attendance on all courses changes to **135**.

9. Change any of the numbers in the range **B4** to **D7** to see the totals automatically change as the cells are edited.

10. Close the workbook without saving.

Exercise 35 - Deleting Cell Contents

Guidelines:

Cell contents are erased by using the keyboard or the menus.

Actions:

1. On a blank worksheet, enter a number into cell **B4** and press **<Enter>**.

2. Erase the entry by clicking on the cell and then pressing the **<Delete>** key.

3. Enter any two numbers into cells **B2** and **B3**.

4. Click on cell **B2** and select **Edit | Clear | Contents**.

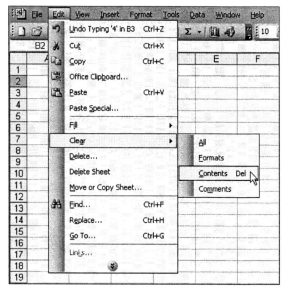

Note: Selecting **All** clears **Contents, Formatting** and **Comments**.

5. The cell is now blank, the contents have been cleared. Clear the **Contents** of cell **B3**.

6. Leave the blank workbook open for the next exercise.

Exercise 36 - In Cell Editing

Guidelines:

Text can be edited directly in a cell: **In Cell Editing**. A cursor is displayed in the cell and the usual movement keys can be used to edit in the cell.

Actions:

1. On a blank worksheet, enter your first name in cell **D6** and complete the entry.

2. Double click in cell **D6**. A cursor is displayed in the cell. If the cursor is not at the end of your name, use the **<End>** key to move to the end. Add a space and type your surname. Complete the entry by pressing **<Enter>**.

3. In cell editing is done either by pressing the **Edit** key **<F2>** or double clicking in the cell. Make **D6** the active cell and press **<F2>**. The cursor is placed in the cell and editing can take place. Click and drag to highlight your first name.

4. Press **<Delete>** to remove it.

5. Press **<Enter>** to complete the entry.

Note: Any part of a cell's contents can be formatted by clicking and dragging during the edit process. Formatting is covered in Section 7.

6. Close the workbook <u>without</u> saving.

Exercise 37 - Revision

1. Open the workbook **Wages**. This is used to calculate the weekly wages for a small company.

2. Column **G** is named **Spare**. Click on cell **G1** and delete the contents. Enter your **Surname** in the cell.

3. Click on cell **G2** enter **5** as your hourly rate of pay.

4. In cell **G3** enter **35** as your normal working hours and in **G4** enter **40** as your worked hours (5 hours of overtime in your first week).

5. Edit your **Tax Code** in cell **G5** to be **350L**. Your **Net Pay** in cell **G11** should be **£161.58**.

6. Close the workbook. Click **No** when prompted to save.

Exercise 38 - Revision

1. Open the workbook **Population**.

2. The population in **China** has risen by half a million. Locate and click on cell **D34**.

3. In the **Formula Bar**, move the cursor after the last **1** in **1139100000**, delete the **1** using the <**Backspace**> key (above <**Enter**>) and type **6** to increase the figure by half a million to **1139600000**. Press <**Enter**> to complete the editing.

4. Type your name into the cell **A1**.

5. Close the workbook and click **No** when asked to save the changes.

Exercise 39 - Revision

Note: The answers for this exercise are listed on page 73.

1. Open the workbook **Widgets Ltd**. This is a spreadsheet for a manufacturing company.

2. The **January Sales** figure has been entered incorrectly. Click on cell **B2** and overtype the correct figure **6125**. How much net profit does the company make in January now?

3. Look at **J14**, the net profit for September, how much is it? The company is starting to make a loss which carries on throughout the rest of the year. As the manager you decide that you can either raise your prices or reduce the amount you spend on Overheads from September onwards.

4. You first try to cut your overheads. Use **In Cell Editing** and change the overhead for September to **4000**. Repeat this through until December. Do you make a profit in December?

5. You next decide to increase your prices from **6** to **7** from September. Overtype the price for September, cell **J3**, with **7** and repeat this through to December. What is the net profit for December?

6. Save the workbook as **Widgets2** and close it.

Section 6

Printing

By the end of this Section you should be able to:

Print Worksheets

Use Print Preview

Use Page Setup

Display and Print Formulas

Exercise 40 - Introduction to Printing

Guidelines:

Printing worksheets produces a hard copy. To print a worksheet, three commands that work together are used:

Print	Controls the print process.
Print Preview	Shows what the worksheet will look like when printed page by page. Used prior to printing and after **Page Setup**.
Page Setup	Controls how the worksheet fits the paper by changing the page settings including landscape, portrait, margins, headers and footers, etc.

When using any of the above commands, the others are available, either via command buttons or buttons on the toolbar.

Actions:

1. Open the workbook **Company**. This shows details of expenses and income of a small company.

Note: Make sure that the appropriate printer is attached to your computer and that it is switched on and is on-line before attempting to print.

2. This is a small worksheet that fits on one piece of paper. The entire worksheet is printed with the default settings using the **Print** button, ⬛, on the toolbar. Click the **Print** button, ⬛. This will automatically start printing with the current settings and print one copy of the worksheet.

*Note: It is customary to **Print Preview** the worksheet before printing, as it may not fit on the paper and **Page Setup** is used to fit the worksheet to the paper. These topics are covered in the next exercises.*

3. Close the workbook <u>without</u> saving any changes.

Exercise 41 - Print Preview

Guidelines:

It is important to see how the worksheet will look on paper before printing it, to make sure that it looks as you expect it to. To do this use **Print Preview**, which shows the layout of the worksheet on the paper - all the pages can be viewed. Make sure the data is not too near the edge of the page, as some printers may not print out all of the data. The worksheet can then be printed from within **Print Preview**.

Actions:

1.   Open the file **Petty Cash**.

2.   Click the **Print Preview** button, [icon], on the toolbar.

Note: An alternative method is to use File | Print Preview.

Example of a Print Preview Button Bar.

3.   **Print Preview** is controlled by the command buttons along the top as shown above.

Note: The Page and number of pages are displayed on the Status Bar.

4.   The mouse pointer becomes a "magnifying glass" when over the "paper". To zoom in on a particular part of the worksheet, move to the required place and click. Click a second time to zoom out again.

5.   Experiment with zooming in and out.

6.   Click the **Close** button, [Close], to close **Print Preview** and return to the worksheet.

7.   Close the workbook <u>without</u> saving.

© CiA Training Ltd 2004

Exercise 42 - Page Setup

Guidelines:

> **Page Setup** allows the appearance of the printed worksheet to be modified.

Actions:

1. Open the workbook **Home Accounts**.

2. **Preview** the workbook to see how it will print.

3. Click the **Setup** button, Setup..., from within **Print Preview**.

Note: Page Setup can also be accessed using the File | Page Setup command with the worksheet displayed.

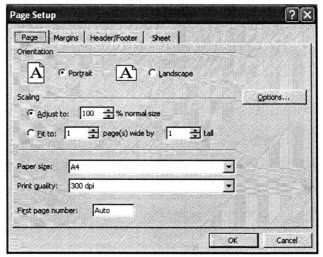

Page Setup with Page tab displayed.

4. The **Page Setup** dialog box has four option tabs, for changing the **Page**, **Margins**, **Header/Footer** and **Sheet** options.

5. Click on the **Page** tab, if it is not selected and select the **Landscape** option. This turns the paper lengthways. Click **OK**. The display now shows how the spreadsheet will appear when printed.

6. Click the **Setup** button and then the **Margins** tab.

continued over

Exercise 42 - Continued

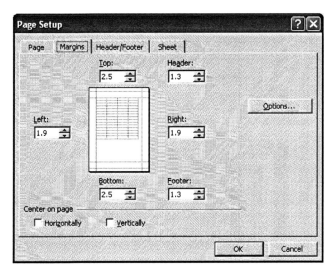

7.   Centre the worksheet on the page by checking the **Horizontally** and **Vertically** boxes under **Center on page**. Note the example in the **Preview** box.

8.   Click **OK** to return to **Print Preview** to see the worksheet with the new settings.

9.   Close **Print Preview** but leave the workbook open for the next exercise.

Note: *The other **Page Setup** tabs, **Header/Footer** is not covered in this guide, **Sheet** is discussed later.*

Exercise 43 - Printing Worksheets

Guidelines:

The **Print** command controls what is printed, how it is printed and number of copies, etc.

Actions:

1. The workbook **Home Accounts** should still be open. Select **File | Print** to display the **Print** dialog box.

*Note: Clicking the **Print** button, [Print...], from within **Print Preview** will also display this dialog box.*

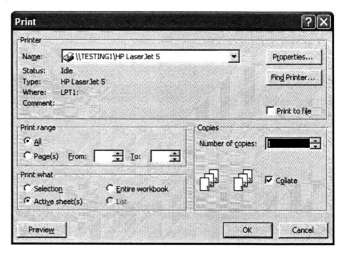

2. Click **OK** to print with the default settings, i.e. 1 copy of the active worksheet. The **Print range** and **Print what** options are not covered in this guide.

3. Close the workbook without saving.

Exercise 44 - Displaying and Printing Formulas

Guidelines:

It is possible to display formulas on a worksheet rather than the results of the formulas. This is very useful when checking for errors on a worksheet.

Columns are widened to display formulas. This means that before printing formulas you should preview the worksheet, to make sure that all of the data fits on to the page. Occasionally you may have to change the page orientation to **Landscape**.

Actions:

1. Open the workbook **Calculations**.

2. To display the formulas select **Tools | Options**.

3. Click on the **View** tab and under **Window options** check **Formulas** then click **OK**. The formulas are displayed and the columns are widened to hold the extra information.

Note: A quicker alternative for switching between the formulas and their results is to press <Ctrl '>, i.e. Ctrl and the key to the left of 1.

4. Switch to the results and then switch back to the formulas using the quick key press method.

5. If the formulas are to be printed, it is normal to display the **Row & column headings** with the formulas so they can be checked. Select **File | Page Setup** and click the **Sheet** tab.

6. Check **Row and column headings** and **Gridlines**. Click **OK**.

7. Use **Print Preview** to see the results. Use **Zoom** if necessary. Change to **Landscape** and centre horizontally and vertically. Click on **OK**.

8. Print the worksheet displaying formulas.

9. Select **File | Page Setup**, click the **Sheet** tab and uncheck **Row and column headings** and **Gridlines**. Click **OK**.

10. Press <Ctrl `> to remove the displayed formulas.

11. Close the workbook <u>without</u> saving.

Exercise 45 - Revision

1. Open the workbook **Home Accounts**.

2. Overtype the contents of cell **A1** with your full name.

3. **Print Preview** the worksheet.

4. Print a copy of the worksheet.

5. Display the formulas. Change the **Page Setup** to **Landscape** and centre the display vertically and horizontally.

6. Print a copy of the worksheet with the formulas displayed.

7. Close the workbook <u>without</u> saving.

Exercise 46 - Revision

1. Open the workbook **Elements**.

2. **Print Preview** the worksheet.

3. Centre the worksheet both **horizontally** and **vertically** on the page.

4. Enter your name in cell **A1**.

5. **Print Preview** the result and print out one copy of the worksheet.

6. Close the workbook <u>without</u> saving.

Exercise 47 - Revision

Note: The answers for this exercise are listed on page 73.

1. Open the workbook **Widgets Ltd**.

2. **Print Preview** the file. How many pages does the worksheet cover?

3. Change the **Page Layout** to **Landscape**. How many pages are there now?

4. Centre the worksheet **vertically** on the page.

5. Enter your name in cell **A16**.

6. **Print Preview** the result and print one copy of the worksheet.

7. Close the workbook <u>without</u> saving.

Section 7

Formatting Cells

By the end of this Section you should be able to:

Format Numbers

Format Currency

Use Alignment

Exercise 48 - Format Cells

Guidelines:

Cells can be **Formatted** in a number of ways. Formatting cells in a worksheet improves its appearance and makes it easier to read and use.

Formatting can change the look of text, text alignment, text colour, number formats, font style, font size, border lines and cell colour. This section will concentrate on alignment, number and currency formatting.

Most of the basic formatting can be added to a worksheet in three ways: by clicking buttons on a toolbar, selecting from menus and using key presses.

Actions:

1. On a blank worksheet select **Format | Cells**.

2. The **Format Cells** dialog box appears, with tabs for the various different formatting options.

3. The **Number** tab is displayed by default. This formats numbers, dates, times and percentages, etc. Click on the **Alignment** tab. This controls how the contents are positioned in the cells.

4. Click on the **Cancel** button to return to the worksheet.

5. Close the workbook <u>without</u> saving.

Exercise 49 - Format Number: Decimal Places

Guidelines:

Numbers can be formatted to be displayed in a variety of ways, such as currency, percentages, etc.
The number formats are as follows:

Type	Description
General	No specific number format
Number	Plain number formats
Currency	Pound signs and decimal places
Accounting	Specialised accounting formats
Date	Various date formats
Time	Various time formats
Percentage	Multiplied by 100 (followed by %)
Fraction	Decimals expressed as fractions
Scientific	Exponent / Mantissa format
Text	Displays formulas, not results
Special	Telephone numbers, N.I. numbers or Postcode
Custom	Allows custom formats to be designed

There are also five or six number formatting buttons on the toolbar. **Currency** format, **Percentage** format, **Comma** format, and **Increase Decimal**, **Decrease Decimal**, and if installed, **Euro** format. Numbers can be shown as **integers** (whole numbers) or with a specified number of decimal places.

Actions:

1. Open the workbook **World Weather**.

2. Click on cell **B5** and drag the mouse to **I16** to highlight all the cells that contain numbers.

3. Select **Format | Cells** and choose the **Number** tab.

continued over

Exercise 49 - Continued

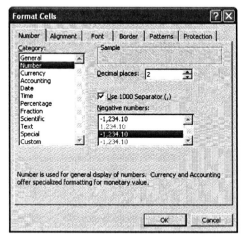

4.   Click on each of the different categories to see the types of number formatting available, then select the **Number** category.

5.   Check that the number of **Decimal places** is **2**.

*Note: The **Sample** box shows the results of the chosen formats applied to the first number in the range of selected cells.*

6.   Click **OK** to apply the chosen formats. All the numbers are now formatted to two decimal places.

7.   Click on cell **B7** and look in the **Formula Bar**. Although the cell contents are formatted to 2 decimal places, the **Formula Bar** shows the actual data that would be used in any calculations (1 decimal place).

8.   To display the numbers as integers, highlight the range **B5:I16**, select **Format | Cells** and the **Number** tab. Change the number of **Decimal places** to **0** and click **OK**.

9.   Change the format of cells **B5** to **I16** back to **2** decimal places.

10. There are also buttons on the toolbar to **Increase Decimal** places, and **Decrease Decimal** places, one for each click. Select the cells **B5:B16** and click the **Decrease Decimal** button,. The numbers are displayed with one decimal place.

Note: After applying number formats, cells may display ########. This means that the number is too big for the cell. Widening columns is covered in the next section.

11. Close the workbook without saving.

Exercise 50 - Format Number: Currency

Guidelines

It is useful to be able to format numbers as currency. This does not always have to be to two decimal places, e.g. if you wanted to show rounded figures, such as £32 rather than £32.23.

Actions:

1. Open the workbook **CD Sales**. Click on cell **C7** and select **Format | Cells | Number**. Examine the selections in the dialog box. Row **7** has been formatted to **0** decimal places. Select **Cancel** to return to the worksheet.

2. Click on cell **C8** and repeat the actions in step 1. The figures in row **8** have been formatted as currency to **2** decimal places. Click **Cancel** again.

3. Click and drag the mouse to highlight cells **C7** to **F7**. Select **Format | Cells | Currency** and in the **Decimal places** area increase the display to **2**. Click **OK**.

4. Close the workbook <u>without</u> saving.

5. Open the workbook **Holiday Cottages**.

6. Click in Cell **B3** and drag the mouse to cell **I14** to select all the cells with numbers.

7. Select **Format | Cells | Currency** to open the Format Cells dialog box.

8. Change the number of decimal places to **0**, and ensure that the currency symbol is **£**. Click **OK** and click away from the selected cells to see the changes. Currency symbols are displayed.

9. Close the workbook <u>without</u> saving.

10. Create a new blank workbook and in column **B** Enter a list of four numbers.

11. Select the numbers and then select **Format | Cells | Currency**. This time select to display the numbers to 2 decimal places. Click **OK**.

12. With the cells still highlighted click the **Decrease Decimal** button, on the toolbar (remember to use the chevrons if it is not visible). Click the same button again to format the numbers to no decimal places.

13. Close the workbook <u>without</u> saving.

Exercise 51 - Alignment

Guidelines:

Aligning means changing the position of cell contents within the cell relative to its edges. Contents can be aligned horizontally or vertically and the orientation may also be changed.

Actions:

1. Open the workbook **Fruit Sales**.

2. Select the range **B3:E3**. There are 3 buttons on the toolbar to align these titles differently: **Align Left**, ▤, **Center,** ▤ and **Align Right,** ▤.

3. Click the **Center** button, ▤. The labels are centred. Click the **Align Right** button, ▤ and the labels are moved to the right.

4. For more alignment options the **Format | Cells** command is used. Highlight the range **A3:E3** and select **Format | Cells** and the **Alignment** tab.

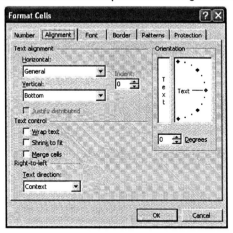

5. The buttons used earlier are the **Horizontal** options. The options in the **Vertical** drop down list allow positions **Top, Center** and **Bottom**. From this drop down list, select **Center**.

6. Click **OK** to apply the formatting. The labels are displayed in the vertical centre of the cells.

7. Close the workbook <u>without</u> saving.

Exercise 52 - Revision

1. Open the workbook **Interest Rates**.

2. The amounts are right aligned, select the range **A4:A11** and centre the range.

3. Select the range **B3:E3** and centre align the cell contents.

4. Select the range **B4:E11** and format as **Currency** with **2** decimal places, with **£** signs added.

5. Enter your name in cell **A13**.

6. Obtain a horizontally centred printed copy of the worksheet to fit on one page.

7. Save the worksheet as **Interest Rates2**.

8. Close the workbook.

Exercise 53 - Revision

1. Open the workbook **Home Accounts**.

2. The range **B1:E1** is currently centred. Select the range and right align it.

3. Select the range **B2:E16** and format as currency but with no decimal places.

4. Change the paper orientation to **Landscape**.

5. Add your name to cell **A18** and print one copy of the worksheet.

6. Close the workbook <u>without</u> saving.

Exercise 54 - Revision

1. Open the workbook **Interest Rates**. This is a table showing the interest received on varying amounts for different interest rates.

2. Highlight the range **B4:E11**, all the interest received figures.

3. Format the cells as currency with a **£** sign and 2 decimal places.

4. Add your name to cell **A13**.

5. Print Preview the worksheet and print one copy.

6. Close the workbook <u>without</u> saving.

Section 8

Formatting Worksheets

By the end of this Section you should be able to:

Change Column Widths
Insert Rows and Columns
Delete Rows and Columns
Hide Rows and Columns

Exercise 55 - Changing Column Widths

Guidelines:

You may sometimes need to change column widths to display the contents of the cells within the columns. A column width is measured using the average number of digits in the standard **font** (the style of text, e.g. **Arial** - the default is **8.43**) and the number of pixels (the tiny dots which make up the screen - the default is **64**). These figures are displayed as the **Adjust Cursor, ✛**, is dragged to the required location.

Actions:

1. Open the workbook **Theatre**.

2. Some of the labels in **Column A** and **Row 2** have been shortened. Move the pointer to the border between **Column A** and **Column B** in the column **Title Bar**. The pointer should change shape to a double arrow, **✛**, the **Adjust Cursor**.

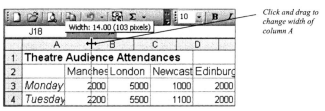

Click and drag to change width of column A

3. Click the mouse button and, with the button still pressed, drag the column border to the right. Drag the column width to **14.00** or **103** pixels. Release the mouse button. This is the easiest way of changing the width of individual columns.

4. An alternative way to change a column width is to use the menus. Click on any cell in **Column C**. Select **Format | Column | Width**. Enter a column width of **20**, then click on **OK**.

5. Move the mouse pointer to the border between **Column B** and **Column C** in the column **Title Bar**. Double click the mouse. The width of column **B** is automatically adjusted to the widest entry in the column.

6. Select **Columns B** to **G** by clicking and dragging across the column headings **B, C, D**, etc.

7. Drag any of the adjust cursors in the range to change all columns to **12.00** units (**89 pixels**). Columns **B** to **G** will be resized to this value.

8. Leave the workbook open for the next exercise.

Exercise 56 - Inserting Columns

Guidelines:

When developing spreadsheets it is inevitable that at some point, room will not have been provided for particular data that is important. Instead of starting again, rows or columns can be inserted.

Columns are inserted to the left of the active cell

It is important to <u>check that all formulas are correct</u> after inserting rows and columns.

Actions:

1. The workbook **Theatre** should still be open. If not, open it.

2. Use **Autosum** in cell **G3** to total **Row 3**.

3. Use the **Fill Handle** to complete the row totals in cells **G4** to **G8**.

4. Another city must be included in the statistics. Click on any cell in **Column D**. Insert a new column for **Belfast** by selecting **Insert | Columns**.

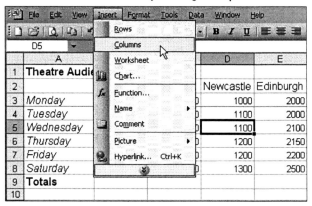

Note: *Columns are best inserted in the middle of a range, inserting at the ends will require the formulas to be adjusted.*

5. Enter the label **Belfast** in cell **D2** and the attendance figures in **column D** as for **Newcastle**. The totals in column **H** are adjusted to include the new numbers (column widths may need reducing to view the worksheet complete).

6. Leave the workbook **Theatre** open for the next exercise.

Exercise 57 - Inserting Rows

Guidelines:

Rows are inserted in a similar way to columns. New rows are inserted above the active cell.

Actions:

1. Open the workbook **Theatre** if not still open from the previous exercise. Thursday matinee attendances have accidentally not been included. As an alternative to the menus right click on the **row heading 7** to display a **Shortcut Menu** and select **Insert**.

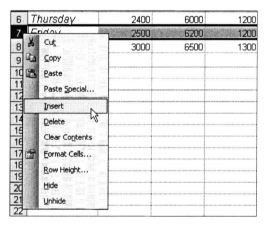

2. Enter **Matinee** in cell **A7**. Enter any numbers across the row in columns **B to G** and copy the formula from **H6** into **H7**.

3. Complete the **Totals** in row **10**.

Note: When rows or columns are inserted, remember to check all the formulas.

4. Enter your name in cell **A12**.

5. Print a copy of the worksheet.

6. Leave the workbook open for the next exercise.

Exercise 58 - Deleting Rows and Columns

Guidelines:

Unwanted rows or columns can be deleted. Deleting a whole row or column is not the same as deleting cell contents.

Actions:

1. The workbook **Theatre** should still be open. If not, open it.

2. Selecting the row number or column letter will allow the deletion of a row or column. Only cities in England are to be included. **Columns D, F and G** are to be deleted. Click on the column heading **D**. Select **Edit | Delete**.

3. Click anywhere in **Column E** (Edinburgh). Select **Edit | Delete**. The **Delete** dialog box is displayed, as the column was not selected first.

4. Select **Entire column**.

5. Click **OK**.

6. Right click on the column **E** heading and select **Delete** from the shortcut menu.

Note: The results in cell formulas can be altered by deleting parts of the worksheet, resulting in errors, indicated by #REF in the cells.

7. Use one of the methods described above to delete row **7**.

8. Print a copy of the worksheet.

9. Close the workbook <u>without</u> saving.

Exercise 59 - Hiding Rows

Guidelines:

When you need to remove sensitive data from view, but do not want to delete it, rows and/or columns of data can be hidden. The calculation of the sheet is unaffected.

Actions:

1. Use the workbook **Wardle Enterprises**. Basic Pay and Overtime rate are not to be displayed.

2. Highlight the complete rows **6** and **7**. Select **Format | Row | Hide**. Rows **6** and **7** have now been hidden.

	A	B	C	D	E	F	G	H	I	J
1	*Payroll*	Jones	Hill	Robson	Wilson	Harris	Spare	Nichols	Chapman	Total
2	Hourly Rate	£9.50	£6.50	£2.75	£2.75	£2.00	£0.00	£1.50	£1.50	£26.50
3	Normal Hours	35	35	40	40	40	0	20	20	230
4	Hours Worked	35	35	40	42	40	0	0	0	192
5	Tax Code	375H	300L	367L	300L	300L	300L	300L	300L	
8	Gross Pay	£332.50	£227.50	£110.00	£118.25	£80.00	£0.00	£30.00	£30.00	£928.25
9	National Ins	£25.43	£15.98	£5.40	£6.14	£2.70	£0.00	£0.00	£0.00	£55.64
10	Income Tax	£65.10	£42.45	£9.86	£15.14	£5.58	£0.00	£0.00	£0.00	£138.12
11	Net Pay	£241.98	£169.07	£94.74	£96.97	£71.72	£0.00	£30.00	£30.00	£734.49
12										
13	National Ins	9								
14	Income Tax	25								
15	Overtime Rate	1.5								

*Rows 6 and 7 are hidden. Note that row 8 still correctly calculates the **Gross Pay**.*

3. To re-display rows **6** and **7**, highlight a range of cells in row 5 to row 8, e.g. **A5:A8** and select **Format | Row | Unhide**.

4. Leave the workbook open for the next exercise.

Exercise 60 - Hiding Columns

Guidelines:

Columns of data can be hidden without affecting calculations in the worksheet.

Actions:

1. Open the workbook **Wardle Enterprises**, if not already open.

2. As **Column G** is not currently assigned to an employee it is to be hidden. Click on the column heading **G** and select **Format | Column | Hide**.

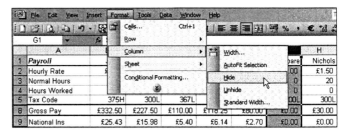

Note: *An alternative method is to right click on the column heading and select **Hide** from the shortcut menu.*

3. To re-display column **G**, select columns **F** to **H**, right click and select **Unhide**.

4. Columns can also be hidden by dragging their border until the column width is zero.

5. Using this method to hide column **D**, place the mouse pointer on the column divider between **D** and **E**. Drag the adjust cursor to the left, carefully, until the column width is 0.00.

Note: *Dragging further left hides multiple columns.*

6. The mouse can also be used to unhide columns (and hidden rows). To the right of a hidden column, display the normal adjust cursor. Move slowly to the right until the cursor changes to a ⁺‖⁺ cursor. Dragging this cursor redisplays the hidden data. Unhide column **D** making it **10.00** units wide.

7. Close the workbook <u>without</u> saving.

Exercise 61 - Revision

1. Open the workbook **Home Accounts**.

2. Insert 3 new columns between the **March** column and the **Total** column.

3. Enter labels in these new columns for **April, May** and **June**.

4. Right align the labels in cells **B1** to **H1**.

5. In **Row 2**, use the **Fill Handle** to complete cells **E2, F2** and **G2**.

6. Click on cell **H2** and notice the formula does not include the newly created columns. Edit the formula to correct this.

7. Copy the amended formula in **H2** to the range **H3** to **H15**.

8. Enter other income as follows: **Apr-200, May-250** and **June-100**.

9. Click in **E4** and use **AutoSum** to calculate the total income for **April**.

10. Complete the totals in cells **F4** and **G4** using any method.

11. The Rent has trebled from April (£240). Enter this amount in the relevant cells.

12. Expenditure is to be cut severely. The car has been sold, therefore no petrol or car costs. There are to be no holidays and the telephone is disconnected. Remove the appropriate rows.

13. Remove the row for **Leisure** too.

14. Complete the rows for **April, May and June. Electricity: 40, Gas: 40, Food: 70** and **Others: 150**.

15. Complete **Row 10, Total Expenses** and **Row 11, Savings**.

16. Hide rows **5** to **9**.

17. Amend the formula in cell **H11** to **=G11** a copy of the previous cell.

18. Insert two rows at the top of the worksheet and enter your name in cell **A1**.

19. Print a copy of the worksheet.

20. Close the workbook <u>without</u> saving.

Exercise 62 - Revision

1. Open **Fruit Sales** and insert three additional rows to display sales for **April, May** and **June.**

2. Enter **April, May** and **June** in cells **A7, A8** and **A9.**

3. Enter some appropriate numbers in columns **B, C** and **D** for the new rows.

4. Click on **B10** and examine the formula. Does it include the new rows? (Answer on page 73).

5. Complete column **E** in rows **7, 8** and **9.**

6. Widen columns **B** to **E** to 10 units.

7. Format all the figures in the range **B4** to **E10** to two decimal places.

8. Format the range **B11** to **E14** to display the currency symbol. (###### shown in any cells indicates that the column needs widening further) and for the display to show 2 decimal places.

9. Centre the fruit titles in row 3 to complete the **Fruit Sales** worksheet.

10. Print a copy of the worksheet.

11. Close the workbook <u>without</u> saving.

Exercise 63 - Revision

1. Open the workbook **Widgets Ltd**. This spreadsheet shows simplified accounts for a small company, displaying income (turnover), spending and net profit.

2. The workers are paid very little and the manager has decided to hide that row. Hide row **6** using the **Format | Row | Hide** command.

3. The manager is only interested in the last 6 months of the year. To hide the first six months, carefully place the mouse cursor between the **G** and **H** in the column border. Drag the adjust cursor to the border between **A** and **B** and release the mouse button to hide the columns.

4. Add your name to cell **A16.**

5. Print a copy for the manager.

6. The manager has decided to include the figures for June. Unhide column **G** and reprint the worksheet.

7. Close the workbook <u>without</u> saving.

Answers

Exercise 8

Step 2	The current workbook is **Book1**.
Step 3	**File, Edit, View, Insert, Format, Tools, Data, Window, Help.**
Step 5	The **ToolTip** is **Save**.

Exercise 13

Step 2	400.
Step 3	**H11, 380.**
Step 7	2 files refer to Holiday Cottages.

Exercise 32

Step 3	129.
Step 4	100.
Step 5	103 in February and 160 in March.
Step7	363.

Exercise 33

Step 2	369,440,000		
Step 3	a) 2,607,400,00	b) 648,800,000	c) 25,160,00

Exercise 39

Step 2	2275.
Step 3	- 200.
Step 4	No, a loss of 1200.
Step 5	900.

Exercise 47

Step 2	2 pages.
Step 3	1 page.

Exercise 62

Step 4	Yes, the rows are included.

Glossary

Active Cell	A single cell that is currently selected.
Alignment	The position of data within a cell.
AutoSum	A function to sum the contents of a range of cells.
Cell Reference	The "address" of any cell in a worksheet, consisting of the letter that identifies the column that the cell is in, and the number of the row that the cell is on.
Delete	To erase the contents of a selected cell or range.
Fill Handle	A cursor used to copy cell contents.
Format	To change the appearance of cell contents.
Formula	A calculation, can use values and/or cell references.
Formula Bar	A bar above the main worksheet area that displays the actual content of the active cell.
Hiding Rows/Columns	To remove from view data which may be sensitive. The data is not deleted and is still available to any calculations that are dependent upon it.
Label	Text entries that describe the contents of areas of the worksheet e.g. column or row titles.
Operator	The basic mathematical operators are + (add), - (subtract), / (divide) and * (multiply).
Overtype	To type new data into a selected cell that already contains existing data. The new data automatically replaces the original.
Range	A group of adjacent cells.
Relative Cell Reference	A default cell reference is said to be a relative reference because it is able to change automatically to refer to any new location to which it is copied.
Sum	The mathematical term for "add".
Values	Numbers that are either entered directly into cells, or created by formulas within cells.
Workbook	A spreadsheet file.
Worksheet	An individual page within a workbook.

Index

Record of Achievement Matrix

This Matrix is to be used to measure your progress while working through the guide. This is a self assessment process, you judge when you are competent. Remember that afterwards there is an assessment to test your competence.

Tick boxes are provided for each feature. 1 is for no knowledge, 2 is for some knowledge and 3 is for competent. A section is only complete when column 3 is completed for all parts of the section.

Tick the Relevant Boxes **1**: No Knowledge **2**: Some Knowledge **3**: Competent

Section	No	Exercise	1	2	3
1 Fundamentals	1	Spreadsheet Principles			
	2	Starting the Program			
	3	The Layout of the Excel Screen			
	4	Menu Bar			
	5	Toolbars			
	6	Worksheet Window			
	7	Closing Excel			
2 Open, Save & Close Workbooks	9	Opening a Workbook			
	10	Moving Around using the Keyboard			
	11	Closing a Workbook			
	12	Saving a Named Workbook			
3 Creating a Worksheet	15	Spreadsheet Structure			
	16	Creating a Spreadsheet			
	17	Starting a New Workbook			
	18	Entering Labels			
	19	Entering Numbers			
	20	Saving a New Workbook			
4 Formulas	24	Introducing Formulas			
	25	Mathematical Operators			
	26	Brackets			
	27	Selecting Cells with the Mouse			
	28	AutoSum			
	29	Using the Fill Handle to Copy			
	30	Copying Formulas			
	31	Relative Addressing			
5 Editing Cells	34	Overtyping			
	35	Deleting Cell Contents			
	36	In Cell Editing			

Tick the Relevant Boxes **1**: No Knowledge **2**: Some Knowledge **3**: Competent

Section	No	Exercise	1	2	3
6 Printing	40	Introduction to Printing			
	41	Print Preview			
	42	Page Setup			
	43	Printing Worksheets			
	44	Displaying and Printing Formulas			
7 Formatting Cells	48	Format Cells			
	49	Format Number: Decimal Places			
	50	Format Number: Currency			
	51	Alignment			
8 Formatting Worksheets	55	Changing Column Widths			
	56	Inserting Columns			
	57	Inserting Rows			
	58	Deleting Rows and Columns			
	59	Hiding Rows			
	60	Hiding Columns			

Other Products from CiA Training

If you have enjoyed using this guide you can obtain other products from our range of over 100 titles. CiA Training Ltd is a leader in developing self-teach training materials and courseware.

Open Learning Guides

Teach yourself by working through them in your own time. Our range includes products for: Windows, Word, Excel, Access, Works, PowerPoint, Project, Lotus 123, Lotus Word Pro, Internet, FrontPage and many more... We also have a large back catalogue of products, including PageMaker, Quattro Pro, Paradox, Ami Pro, etc. please call for details.

ECDL & ECDL Advanced

We produce accredited training materials for the European Computer Driving Licence (ECDL) qualification, for both the Standard and Advanced syllabus. In 2001 we became one of the first companies in the world to obtain accreditation for the ECDL Advanced modules.

CLAIT Plus

Have you enjoyed doing New CLAIT? Well why not go one step further and take the CLAIT Plus qualification. Materials are now available which follow the same format as our successful New CLAIT material.

e-Quals

To follow the success of our other resources, we have further expanded the courseware portfolio to include training materials for the City & Guilds e-Quals qualification. Specifically designed to steer the user around the features needed to pass the e-Quals assessments.

Trainer's Packs

Specifically written for use with tutor led I.T. courses. The trainer is supplied with a trainer guide (step by step exercises), course notes (for delegates), consolidation exercises (for use as reinforcement) and course documents (course contents, pre-course questionnaires, evaluation forms, certificate template, etc). All supplied on CD with the rights to edit and copy the documents.

Purchasing Options

The above publications are available in a variety of purchasing options; as single copies, class sets and or site licences. However, Trainer's Packs are only available as site licences.

Conventional Tutor Led Training

CiA have been successfully delivering classroom based I.T. training throughout the UK since 1985. New products are constantly being developed; please call to be included on our mailing list. Information about all these materials can be viewed at *www.ciatraining.co.uk*.

Notes